THE QUEENSLAND COURT SURVIVAL GUIDE

By

Dave Abrey

FIRST EDITION

To my parents, who always taught me right from wrong,
and to never judge those who confuse the two.

Injustice anywhere is a threat to justice everywhere.

– Martin Luther King Jr. –

CONTENTS

PART 1
WELCOME

Who Should Read This Book?

This book is short and can be read in about an hour. But even though it's short, it is full of useful information designed to remove as much stress as possible for those who must appear in court.

However, I have not written this book for everyone, and I don't want to waste your time if this is not the right book for you. I have written this book for a specific audience and, therefore, it might not be what you are looking for.

This book will be perfect for you if:

- The police have charged you with a traffic or criminal offence in Queensland;
- You must appear in a Queensland Magistrates Court; and
- You are considering pleading guilty.

This book will also be helpful if you have to appear in court for any other reason, such as family law proceedings. A lot of the information will still be relevant for you.

This book will also be a useful guide for anyone who must appear in a court outside of Queensland. Some procedures in those courts may be slightly different from what happens in Queensland, however. Therefore, you should seek legal advice to confirm what steps you might need to take when appearing in a court outside Queensland.

This book can also help anyone who has criminal charges in a District or Supreme Court. In Queensland, all criminal charges start in Magistrates Courts regardless of whether they end up in a District or Supreme Court. Therefore, this guide will help you through the initial stages of your court case and beyond, no matter which court your case will be finalised in.

Lastly, I have written this book for anyone who is considering pleading guilty. It is beyond the scope of this book to discuss the procedures for going to trial, as this is a far more lengthy and complex process. However, this book is still useful if you decide to plead not guilty and go to trial as many of the topics discussed are still relevant. If you are thinking about going to trial, I strongly recommend that you seek legal advice.

You will see that I have not mentioned anything about whether you have a lawyer or not. If you have hired a lawyer to represent you, they can answer all your questions and explain the procedures – this is one of the many benefits of hiring a lawyer.

However, even if you have already hired a lawyer to represent you, you will still benefit from this book. Unfortunately, some lawyers do not take the time to carefully explain the court process to their clients. As a result, their clients remain confused about what is required when going to court. For this reason, this book will also be helpful even if you have hired a lawyer to represent you.

I am confident that you will find value within these pages and feel much more optimistic about your case once you finish reading this book.

Introduction

Going to court is stressful. For many people, it will be the most stressful experience of their lives.

Many people have genuine concerns about their case, such as:

- What will the outcome of my case be?
- Will I be found guilty?
- Will I go to jail?
- Will I lose my driver's licence, causing me to lose my job?
- However, these are not the only concerns that people face when going to court.

Sometimes, it is simply the fear of the unknown about the court process itself that causes concern. They don't know when to appear in court or what to do when they get there. They don't know what they should wear or whether they can bring a support person with them.

Some people get panic attacks at the thought of speaking in court because they're anxious that they might say the wrong thing and upset the Magistrate.

For others, it might be the embarrassment about appearing in court and the potential damage it could have on their reputation.

There are many, many reasons why a person might feel worried about going to court.

I have been practising criminal law for nearly two decades, and I have represented everyone from police officers to surgeons to homeless people battling drug addictions. Almost every single client I have worked with has felt some type of stress about his or her case.

This is why I decided to write this book, the Queensland Court Survival Guide.

Even though I can't address every single concern that a person may have about going to court, I have tried to discuss as many as I reasonably can.

To do this, I have laid this book out in six sections.

Part One of this book is this introductory section. By the end of this part, you will have a good understanding about what you can expect to learn from this book and whether it is the right book for you.

Part Two examines how the courts in Queensland are set up. This information is helpful as it will give you an idea about where your case fits within the Queensland justice system.

In Part Three, we explore the sentencing process in Queensland by going through sentences that a Magistrate can impose in a Magistrates Court.

Part Four looks at what steps you should be taking before you go to court. By following these steps, you will be doing yourself a big favour by making sure you are as prepared as possible when you appear in court.

Next, Part Five outlines what you need to know for when you arrive at court and when you actually appear in front of the Magistrate. This information will help you get through the day with the least amount of stress.

Lastly, Part Six discusses the steps you might need to take once your court case has finished. It is important not to overlook these final steps as there can be severe consequences if you fail to do what's required.

At the end of the book, I have also answered a number of frequently asked questions that I am often asked.

By opening this book, you have already taken a big step towards protecting yourself throughout the court process. You will still have a lot of work ahead of you, but you have given yourself a head start.

I recommend you grab a highlighter, pen and paper and make notes as you read. If you have any questions or comments, feel free to reach out to me at help@harperfinch.com.au and if you want to discuss how I can help with your case, we can arrange an obligation-free chat.

Good luck!

Dave

PART 2
QUEENSLAND COURTS

The Structure of Queensland Courts

Courthouses in Queensland perform many vital roles for the community.

Just some of their functions include:

- Helping members of the public resolve disputes between each other
- Handling personal family issues that arise, including divorce and child custody arrangements
- Managing cases where a person is facing criminal charges
- Settling lawsuits between competing companies.
- There is not one single courthouse, however, that deals with all wthe above functions.

In Queensland, different types of courts deal with different types of cases. For example, the Family Court of Australia deals with matters which (unsurprisingly) involve family law cases. As a result, a Family Court will never deal with cases that involve neighbourhood disputes.

It is useful to understand how the courts are structured and their different roles. However, to avoid potentially wasting your time, I will only explain how Queensland's criminal law courts operate as these are the ones that will apply to you, since you are reading this book.

Queensland's Criminal Courts

There are four levels of courts in Queensland which handle criminal cases.

These are:

- Magistrates Courts
- District Courts
- Supreme Courts
- The Court of Appeal

These courts are arranged in a hierarchy, with each level of court having different powers and responsibilities. As can be seen from the following diagram, the lowest level of courthouse is the Magistrates Court. The next level up is the District Court, then the Supreme Court and finally the Court of Appeal.

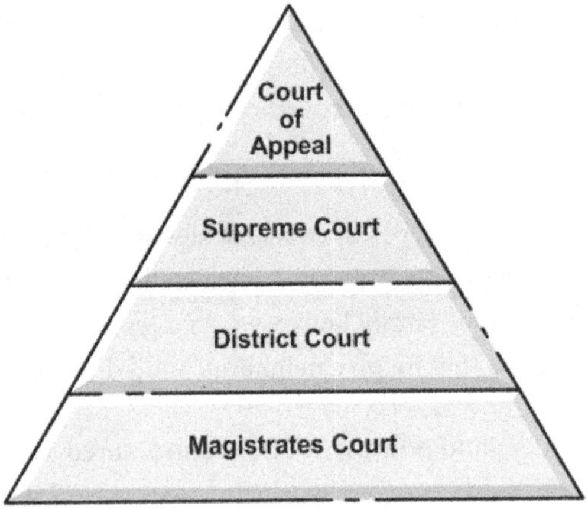

All criminal cases start in a Magistrates Court, but if they are serious enough, they will be transferred to a District or Supreme Court at a later stage. This transfer process is beyond the scope of this book, but you can seek legal advice to learn more.

I will now go through each courthouse in order.

The Magistrates Court

The lowest level of courthouse in Queensland is the Magistrates Court. It does not mean, however, that they are the least essential courthouse. In fact, Magistrates Courts deal with 95% of all criminal cases in Queensland.

A single Magistrate runs each courtroom in a Magistrates Court (but there may be several courtrooms, and therefore several Magistrates, in a courthouse building). The Magistrate is assisted in court by a court Clerk who provides administrative support for the Magistrate.

Magistrates Courts only have the power to deal with less serious criminal offences. These can include simple traffic offences such as drink driving and some cases involving drugs, assaults and stealing.

Since the Magistrates Court is the lowest in the court hierarchy, their sentencing powers are also more limited. For example, a Magistrate generally cannot sentence an offender to more than three years' imprisonment for a single offence. If a more severe punishment is anticipated, the case will be transferred to a higher court (usually a District Court).

All criminal cases start in a Magistrates Court, even if they ultimately end up in a District or Supreme Court. Therefore, it does not mean that your case will remain in a Magistrates Court just because that is where your case started.

There are currently 131 Magistrates Courts in Queensland.

The District Court

The District Court deals with more serious criminal cases, including rape, armed robbery and serious fraud offences. It also hears appeals from the Magistrates Court (we will briefly look at appeals later in this book).

Unlike Magistrates Courts, which are run by a single Magistrate, each District Court courtroom is run by a single Judge.

A significant difference with the Magistrates Courts is how a District Court handles trials. In a Magistrates Court, a single Magistrate will hear the trial and decide whether a person is guilty or not and what sentence to impose. In District Courts, most trials are heard in front of a 12-person jury who determine a person's guilt or innocence. It is then up to the Judge to determine the appropriate sentence.

There are currently 38 District Courts in Queensland.

The Supreme Court

The Supreme Court deals with the most serious criminal cases in Queensland, such as murder and drug trafficking.

Like District Courts, Supreme Courts are also run by Judges, and trials are decided by juries.

There are currently 11 Supreme Courts in Queensland.

The Court of Appeal

The Court of Appeal is not, in fact, a separate court – it is a division of the Supreme Court. Unlike all the lower courts, which are run by a single Judge or Magistrate, the Court of Appeal is run by three or five Supreme Court judges.

This court has a very limited function, which is to hear all District and Supreme Court appeals. In other words, its purpose is to decide whether a lower court made the right decision about a person's guilt or innocence, the punishment that was imposed, or a combination of both.

As a result, the Court of Appeal does not hear original cases and nor does it have a jury.

In relation to the powers available, the Court of Appeal can:

1. Dismiss an appeal and confirm that the lower court was correct, which means that nothing changes; or
2. Allow the appeal and then either make its own order, or send the case back to the lower court for it to be heard again.

The Layout of a Courtroom

When you enter a courtroom for the first time, it is likely to be quite overwhelming. Fortunately, almost all courtrooms have a similar layout, as illustrated in the following picture.

You will most likely enter the courtroom from the back of the room. You will see that there are seats available for members of the public to sit. This area is known as the "Public Gallery", and you will sit here while waiting for the court to hear your case.

The Magistrate will sit at the opposite end of the room. This area is known as the "Bench" and is usually raised higher than the rest of the courtroom. This not only allows the Magistrate to look around the courtroom more easily, but it also gives the impression of authority.

The "Bar Table" is in front of the Public Gallery and faces the Magistrate. The Police Prosecutor will usually be sitting on the right side of the table, and you will sit on the left side when your name is called (usually by the Police Prosecutor).

If a lawyer is representing you, they will sit next to you at the table and will guide you through the process of what to do while inside the courtroom.

The Roles of the People Inside the Courtroom

When you appear in Court, it is helpful to understand who will also be appearing in your case and what their roles are.

Even though most Magistrates Courts are crowded with other people who are also due to appear in Court, the only people you really need to worry about are the following:

- The Magistrate
- The Court Clerk

- The Police Prosecutor
- Defence lawyers

I will go through each of these roles in turn.

The Magistrate

The Magistrate is the most important person in the courtroom – apart from yourself, of course!

Magistrates have a wide range of powers and responsibilities when in Court. The most relevant of these is the power to punish you.

The Magistrate, however, cannot just randomly decide how to punish you. They will hear submissions from the Police Prosecutor about your case and then from you or your lawyer.

They will also read any material that has been provided by the Prosecutor or you/your lawyer.

Once the Magistrate has heard the various submissions and considered all the documents, they will consider all these factors (along with the relevant laws) when deciding how to punish you.

Since it is crucial to make a good impression on the Magistrate, I provide my clients with a list of documents to prepare or other steps to take so that the Magistrate reduces what the punishment would have otherwise been. In many cases, this can make the difference between whether someone goes to jail or not.

Court Clerk

The Court Clerk is the Magistrate's assistant. They will either be sitting to the side of, or in front of, the Magistrate.

The Clerk has many responsibilities, but their primary role is to support the Magistrate by taking care of the administrative tasks while in Court. They will find the Magistrate's files, enter details into the Court's records, and take care of any paperwork submitted in Court.

The Police Prosecutor

The Prosecutor is a member of the Queensland Police Service. The Prosecutor provides the Magistrate with the allegations of the offence, along with any traffic or criminal histories.

Prosecutors also often make submissions to the Magistrate about what they think the appropriate sentence should be.

Be aware that the Prosecutors who appear in Court are not the same police officers who charged you. The police officers who charged you would have prepared a report about your case, which they forward to the relevant Prosecutors' office. Often, this means that the court Prosecutor knows nothing about your case until they appear in court on the day of your court appearance.

Even though it might feel like the Prosecutors are "the enemy", the truth is that most Prosecutors are simply presenting the information that has been provided to them by the arresting officers. It is unlikely that anything they say or do in relation to your case is personal.

Defence Lawyers

If you have decided to hire a defence lawyer, they will appear in Court with you to do all the talking on your behalf. They are responsible for presenting your case to make you look more favourable to the Magistrate. They will explain to the Magistrate how you ended up committing the offence and why the sentence should be reduced. In addition, they will be able to refer to the laws that will help you receive a better outcome.

Many people appear in Court without a defence lawyer; however, they often regret this decision later. An experienced lawyer knows how to present valuable information to the Magistrate. They will also likely have experience appearing in front of the same Magistrate sentencing you. This means that your lawyer will be able to use this knowledge to your advantage by making submissions in a way that the Magistrate appreciates.

PART 3
SENTENCES IN QUEENSLAND

It is likely that one of your biggest concerns about going to court is what punishment you will receive.

In this chapter, we review the types of sentences that a Magistrate can impose so that you have an understanding about what the consequences might be.

Punishments That a Magistrate May Impose

There is a wide range of penalties or sentences that a Magistrate can impose.

To decide what the appropriate punishment should be, the Magistrate will consider a variety of factors, including:

- The maximum and minimum penalties that apply to the offence
- The nature of the offence, including any physical, mental or emotional harm suffered by the victim
- Your character, age and intellectual capacity
- How common the offence is
- Your cooperation with the police during their investigations
- Whether you pleaded guilty or were found guilty after a trial
- Your previous criminal history
- Any other particular issues that either work in your favour or against you.

Once the Magistrate has considered all these factors, they will impose a punishment which includes one or more of the following penalties.

Good Behaviour Bond

A good behaviour bond is simply a promise that you make to the Court that you will not commit any further offences for a fixed period. You make this promise by signing a document called a recognisance.

When imposing a good behaviour bond, the Magistrate will let you know how long the bond will go for. In addition, the Magistrate will tell you what the consequences will be if you breach the bond by committing an offence during the period it runs for. Usually, the punishment for breaching a bond is a fine.

Fines

Fines in Queensland are based on a system that uses Penalty Units as a way to determine the amount of the fine.

Each Penalty Unit is a set monetary amount that the Government decides and is used to calculate what the actual fine is. At the time of writing this book, a Penalty Unit is worth $166.90.

To understand how this system works, let's take an example where an offence is punishable by a fine of up to 20 Penalty Units. In this case, the maximum fine would be 20 x $166.90 which is $3,338.00.

However, a Magistrate can impose a fine that is less than the maximum and does not need to set a fine equal to a certain amount of Penalty Units. In other words, the Magistrate can impose a fine of $100 even though this is less than a single Penalty Unit. The Penalty Units are simply an easy way to calculate maximum and minimum fines.

If you are given a fine as your punishment, the Magistrate may give you a specific time to pay the fine. If you fail to pay the fine within the required time, you could be given a jail sentence as a punishment. For example, the Magistrate may say, "You are fined $500 with one month to pay, in default 7 days imprisonment." Here, you have one month to pay the $500 fine, but you could end up being jailed for 7 days if you fail to pay within the month.

Alternatively, the Magistrate might refer the fine to the State Penalties Enforcement Registry ("SPER") for collection. This will allow you to enter into an instalment plan to pay off the fine. If your fine is referred to SPER, you may have to pay an enforcement fee in addition to your fine.

Compensation/Restitution

If your offending caused someone to suffer financial loss, the Magistrate may order that you pay restitution. This is a sum of money that repays the victim for their financial loss.

For example, suppose you broke someone's window when trespassing. In that case, you could be ordered to pay the victim a sum of money to cover the costs of repairing the window.

Restitution is not intended to punish you for your actions. Instead, it requires you to fix the damage that you caused.

Alternatively, if a person suffered some form of pain or suffering, a Magistrate could make a compensation order. The victim isn't required to demonstrate financial loss, but they must provide evidence of suffering in another form.

Compensation orders are often imposed in assault cases where the victim suffered physical pain and discomfort due to the assault. In these cases, it is common for Magistrates to order the offender to pay the victim a sum of money as compensation.

Importantly, a Magistrate can impose both a restitution order and a compensation order at the same time. In the above example of an assault offence, the victim might have suffered pain and suffering but may also have needed to take time off from work due to their injuries. In this situation, a Magistrate could order both compensation for the pain and suffering and restitution for the victim's lost income.

When making an order for compensation or restitution, the Magistrate should state:

- How much needs to be paid;
- Who to pay it to;
- When it needs to be paid by; and
- How to make the payment.

Like fines, a Magistrate can refer restitution and compensation orders to SPER for collection.

Probation

Probation is a community-based court order that puts a person on a specific list of conditions. In other words, the person will need to comply with the probation order conditions to comply with their sentence. If the person breaches any of the conditions, they may be sent to jail or given another form of punishment.

All probation orders will have a standard set of conditions that must be followed. These mandatory conditions include:

- Not committing further offences during the period of the probation order
- Reporting to a probation officer when required
- Getting permission before leaving Queensland
- Notifying their probation officer if they change where they live or work.

In some instances, a Magistrate may impose additional conditions requiring the person to attend counselling or submit to drug tests.

The period of a probation order can be anywhere from six months to 3 years.

Community Service

Like probation, community service is a community-based order; however, a community service order's focus is to require the person to give back to the community through unpaid work.

A person can do many different types of work. The kind of work given will depend on the person's circumstances, such as where they live, their ability to travel and any health issues that they may have. It could include, for example, doing unpaid work in a warehouse or a restaurant.

A community service order can be from 40 to 240 hours and, in most cases, must be completed within one year.

Imprisonment

You might think that imprisonment doesn't need much explaining. However, sentencing a person to prison can often be an incredibly complex process. Many different factors must be taken into account.

First, there is the type of prison sentence that a court should impose. Most people know that imprisonment requires a person to go to jail; however, there are situations where a person is given a prison sentence but does not actually go to jail. This can be through a suspended jail sentence or an order of immediate parole. Although it is beyond the scope of this book to explain what these sentences involve, the main function is to allow a person to remain in the community despite being sentenced to imprisonment.

In addition to the type of jail sentence that a court should impose, the court will also need to consider other factors such as:

- How much time the person has already served in jail (if any);
- Whether there are any mandatory periods of jail that must be imposed; and
- What impact a jail sentence might have on other penalties that have already been imposed.

Given the complexity of jail sentences, I strongly encourage you to get legal advice if you think you might be at risk of imprisonment.

Recording of a Conviction

For many people going to court, their biggest concern is whether a criminal conviction will be recorded against their name.

If a conviction is recorded on your criminal history, you may need to disclose this to employers as well as to embassies when applying to travel overseas.

Magistrates have the power to record convictions for most offences. However when a Magistrate gives a prison sentence, a conviction must be recorded – this is mandatory, no exceptions.

If a Magistrate does have the choice to impose a conviction, the law says that they have to consider the following:

- The nature of the offence;
- The offender's character and age;
- The impact that a conviction will have on the offender's:
- Economic or social wellbeing; or
- Chances of finding employment.

Typically, when an individual is found guilty of an offence, a Magistrate will enter a conviction.

Imagine you're trying to prevent a conviction from being entered on your record. In this situation, you must persuade the Magistrate that a conviction should not be entered. It is not enough just to say that it could have an impact on you – you will need to argue why it would specifically affect you.

If you have a lawyer representing you, your chances of not having a conviction recorded is much greater. This is because we know what arguments to use to give you the best chance of no recorded conviction.

Licence Disqualification

If you are pleading guilty to an offence involving a vehicle, there is a real risk that your driver's licence will be disqualified.

Many traffic offences, such as drink driving, dangerous driving or unlicensed driving, specify how long a Magistrate can disqualify you. This period depends on the type of offence, the type of licence you held at the time of the offence (Open, Provisional, Learner, etc.) and your previous traffic history. These factors will tell the Magistrate any maximum or minimum disqualification periods that can apply.

Once the Magistrate knows the appropriate range, they will then consider all the other circumstances of your case to determine how long the actual disqualification should be.

Even if the offence doesn't require a mandatory licence disqualification, the Magistrate has the power to disqualify your licence simply because the offence involved the use of a motor vehicle. The example I often explain to my clients is where someone commits a drive-by shooting offence. Even though the principal offence is that the person used a weapon to shoot at someone, their licence can be disqualified because they were in a vehicle at the time.

Unfortunately, many people are unaware that they face the loss of their driver's licence when they get to court. This usually happens when they are unrepresented or have not obtained legal advice beforehand. They then get a shock when they plead guilty and end up having to surrender their driver's licence to the Police Prosecutor while still in court. This is just another reason why it is important to seek legal advice before appearing in court.

In some circumstances, it may be possible to apply for a special restricted licence. Such a licence will allow you to keep driving for specific purposes, even though your licence is otherwise disqualified. Therefore, if your licence is essential to you for any reason (work, family, etc.), I strongly encourage you to speak with a lawyer before going to court.

Offender Levy

The Offender Levy is an administrative fee that helps to pay the costs of running the courthouses, law enforcement, etc. Every person that is convicted of an offence in the Magistrates, District or Supreme Courts must pay the Offender Levy.

At the time of writing, the Offender Levy in the Magistrates Court is currently $142.80.

The Offender Levy is not, strictly speaking, a punishment that a Magistrate can impose. The Magistrate has no power over whether a person must pay the levy or not. They also have no power over how much the levy should be. The Government imposes the levy, and it cannot be changed or waived.

However, since it is part of the consequences of being convicted of an offence in Queensland, it is useful for you to know that you will most likely have to pay the levy after your case is finalised.

You will have the option of paying the Offender Levy on the day of court. Alternatively, you can pay it through the State Penalties Enforcement Registry.

PART 4
BEFORE COURT

Now that you hopefully have a better understanding of how the court system works, it's time to start preparing for your case.

This chapter outlines several steps that you can take before going to court. Some steps are much more important than others, and some won't apply to you at all. Furthermore, there might be some other steps that you should take that I have not described below.

Get Legal Advice

If you face a traffic or criminal offence, the very first thing you should do is to seek legal advice.

There are many reasons why it's essential to speak with a lawyer about your case. Some of these reasons include:

1. A lawyer will give you advice about the seriousness of the charge, the likely punishment and so on;
2. They may be able to negotiate the charge to downgrade the seriousness or, in some cases, to have the charge dropped completely;
3. A lawyer can also take a lot of the pressure off you by guiding you through the whole process.

Do not delay contacting a lawyer. I can't count the number of times people have contacted me after they didn't seek legal advice early enough and ended up with a bad outcome at court. Some options are time-sensitive, which is why getting advice early gives you the widest range of choices.

A typical example of this is where someone has been charged with drink driving. Ordinarily, that person may be able to apply for a "work licence", which allows them to keep driving for work purposes despite being disqualified by the court for the drink-driving offence. The problem is that a person needs to apply for a work licence while pleading guilty to the offence. Many people contact me in distress after pleading guilty, being disqualified, and now needing a work licence. At that point, it's too late and there's nothing I can do.

If you want legal advice, you have a few options.

First, you can contact a private lawyer. If your issue is simple, they might resolve it with a brief phone call. If your case is complex or you have many questions, book an appointment. There will usually be a fee for the appointment, but the benefits should easily outweigh the cost.

If you decide not to contact a private lawyer for any reason, you can contact Legal Aid Queensland or a local Community Legal Centre. These organisations typically have someone to answer your questions. However, in the majority of cases, they are not permitted to provide legal representation or appear in court on your behalf.

Whether you choose to speak with a private lawyer or a community lawyer, they will want to know as much about your case as possible.

Therefore, you should collect any relevant paperwork you have, including any documents given to you by the police. It would also be helpful if you wrote a summary of your version of events regarding the offence. Lastly, you should write down a list of the questions you may want to ask, ensuring that you get all the information you need to decide how to proceed further.

Here are some possible questions you could consider asking:

- How long will my case take?
- What punishment might I receive?
- How should I prepare for court?
- How much would a lawyer cost me?

Research Your Charge

Suppose you were unwell, and a doctor told you that you had a serious disease. In that case, I assume that you would want to know as much about your diagnosis as possible. You'd likely be interested in learning the disease's name, its symptoms, possible treatments, and other relevant information.

If you have been charged with a traffic or criminal offence, it should be no different.

At the very minimum, you should want to know the following information:

1. The charge(s) you are facing

   It is worrying how often someone contacts me for legal advice or representation but can't tell me what charges they face. I am in no way trying to criticise them – I understand just how confusing the criminal justice system can be for many people.

Not only that, but many people are charged with offences while under the influence of drugs or alcohol, or in circumstances where they are suffering from severe anxiety due to the presence of police. In these situations, it is common for people's memories to be hazy and, therefore, not remember what offences the police charged them with.

You should, therefore, make sure that you at least know what charges you are facing.

2. The penalties available

For most people, their biggest concern about going to court is the Magistrate's penalty.

As discussed previously in this book, Magistrates cannot randomly choose what punishments they will impose. There are many factors that they will take into account. The main factor that they must follow is any maximum or minimum penalties that a sentence carries. If they impose a punishment that is less than the minimum, or more than the maximum, the penalty is unlawful, and it is possible that either you will need to be resentenced at a later date, or the sentence could be appealed by either yourself or the Prosecutors.

Let us take an example. In Queensland, a common assault charge carries a maximum sentence of imprisonment of three years. This means that a Magistrate can imprison a person for a common assault charge for up to 3 years. If the Magistrate imposed a four-year sentence, that sentence would be unlawful, and that person would need to be resentenced.

There is no minimum sentence in this example, which means that the Magistrate could impose any sentence of fewer than three years imprisonment, including fines, probation or community service.

Let's take another example.

If you are convicted of a drug driving offence, a licence disqualification is unavoidable – the Magistrate has no choice but to disqualify your licence. Depending on the specific charge and the type of driver's licence you hold, the minimum licence disqualification will be stated in the legislation. If a Magistrate ordered a licence disqualification that is shorter than what is required by law, it would be an unlawful sentence and could be appealed by the police.

By knowing the range of sentences that a Magistrate can impose, it will give you an idea about what the possible punishment might be.

Hopefully, after reading through the above, you will understand why it's essential to research your charge beforehand.

You should, however, be careful about how you research your charge. It can be dangerous to rely on Dr Google for medical advice. It is also harmful to turn to Google for legal advice.

A lot of information available on the internet is outdated or simply plain wrong. Also, many law firm websites provide information that is meant to persuade you to hire them – not to provide information and advice honestly and reliably.

The starting point for your research should be the paperwork that was given to you by the police when they charged you. This paperwork almost always includes a Notice to Appear, which is a slip of paper telling you your charge(s); your court date; and which courthouse you are required to attend.

However, the Notice to Appear usually includes just a very brief name of the offence. For example, it may state the offence as "UIL" instead of "driving under the influence of liquor". It therefore only provides you with limited information.

The next step, then, is to get a copy of the police report from the Prosecutors. This report is also known as a "QP9" which is simply the form number. You can usually collect this from the Prosecutors at court on your first court appearance. You can then ask for an adjournment to seek legal advice (see the FAQ for information on applying for an adjournment).

The police report provides details of the offence that you have been charged with. In fact, it is the exact same document that the Prosecutors will read to the Magistrate when describing the details of your offence. By obtaining the police report beforehand, you will not be caught by surprise by the Prosecutor telling the Magistrate details about your case that you weren't aware of or disagree with completely.

(Note – in my practice, I always obtain a copy of the police report before my clients' first court date, which usually avoids the need to return to court a second time.)

Once you have obtained the police report (and assuming that you haven't hired a lawyer to do this for you), you can research your case online. The best place to do this is to go straight to the legislation. However, given how confusing legislation can be, you should be able to find some basic details from reputable legal resource websites.

Decide How You Want to Plead

Once you have researched your charge, you will need to decide how you want to plead.

As explained earlier, I have written this book on the assumption that you are pleading guilty in court (even though this book is still helpful for those who are pleading not guilty).

However, choosing how to plead is often not easy, and you should not just automatically assume that you should plead guilty. You should answer many different questions before you can confidently decide whether to plead guilty or not guilty.

For example, let's again pretend that you've been charged with drink driving. You might assume that you should plead guilty because you were breath-tested in your car and you were over the limit.

However, let's pretend that you were actually asleep in a parked car on the side of the road when the police approached you. In that case, a charge of "drink driving" is probably not correct if you were not driving. In that case, you might want to consider challenging the charge by going to trial, or you could look at sending a submission to the Prosecutors.

If you have a lawyer representing you, they will be able to review the police report and take your instructions about what happened. They should then give you some advice about whether you should consider pleading guilty or not guilty.

The ultimate decision, however, is up to you. Your lawyer cannot tell you what you should do – they can only explain your options to you and, in some cases, provide recommendations.

Get Character References

When you appear in court for sentencing, you want the Magistrate to know that you are a good person and that this offending was out of character.

When I appear in Court with a client, I always spend considerable time explaining to the Magistrate why they should not punish my client too harshly. I do this by focusing on the positive parts of my clients' lives, whether it be their employment, contributions to the community or the steps they have taken towards rehabilitation.

The Magistrate, however, understands that it is my responsibility to say good things about my clients. For this reason, character references can make a big difference.

A character reference is simply a letter written on behalf of a person by someone who knows them well. It can be from employers, family members, friends, or other close associates.

For a character reference to have the biggest impact, however, certain guidelines apply. For example, the person writing the reference should confirm that they know they are writing a reference for a person who is appearing in court for an offence. There are also certain things that they should or shouldn't say in their reference.

I have a comprehensive guide that I send out to all my clients to help them obtain powerful character references. If you would like a copy, contact us at help@harperfinch.com.au.

Complete a Road Safety Education Course

If you are going to court for a driving offence, you should strongly think about doing a road safety education course.

I'm not talking about the courses where you physically learn how to drive in different weather conditions. I'm referring to courses that have been specifically created to improve drivers' attitudes to driving. They usually cover a wide range of traffic offences and provide helpful information and statistics to improve each participant's road safety awareness.

There are many different courses available, and they can be done either online or in-person. You should be able to find several by doing a quick internet search.

Drug/Alcohol/Anger Counselling

Many people commit offences because of drugs, alcohol, or anger (or a combination of these).

If you think you fall into one of these categories, you may benefit from seeking counselling to deal with any issues you have with these negative influences.

There are two significant benefits from doing so.

First, it can prevent you from committing further offences because of those negative influences.

Second, it will impress the Magistrate. It will show that you have identified the underlying cause of your offending and have taken steps to address that cause.

There are too many counselling services out there to list here, but a good starting point would be to talk to your GP. If you feel comfortable doing so, you can explain your situation to your GP, who can then write a referral for you to seek professional help.

Seek Counselling

Going to court can be an incredibly stressful process. Not only that, but it can also go for an extended time (some cases can go for two years or more).

The stress of going to court can impact your mental health, your employment and your relationships with family and friends. You must look after yourself and those around you while you go through this process.

For this reason, I recommend that you seek counselling which may involve seeing a therapist, psychologist, or a psychiatrist. You will have someone to talk to who will not judge you for what you have done and, importantly, they will also be able to provide you with mental tools to help you cope with going to court.

If you speak to your GP, you may qualify for a Mental Health Care Plan, meaning Medicare will partially subsidise your counselling sessions.

Importantly, your counsellor may also be able to write a letter for the court. This letter will provide details about the support you have been receiving and any factors that may have contributed to your offending. This information often makes a significant impact in court.

Arrange a Support Person

As I have stated several times, going to court is an incredibly stressful experience for most people. I have personally appeared in court with thousands of people, and I have seen just how intimidating the court process can be for ordinary members of the community.

For this reason, I recommend that my clients bring a support person to court with them. This can be a family member, a close friend or anyone else that can provide emotional support.

Depending on the courthouse, your support person may not be allowed into the courtroom with you. You will, however, appreciate someone waiting with you beforehand and then available afterwards while you decompress.

Research the Courthouse

As I will discuss in the next part, you do not want to turn up to court late.

One of the easiest ways this can happen is because you don't know where the courthouse is or waste time trying to find a carpark nearby.

To avoid this, you should spend a few minutes researching the courthouse in which you need to appear.

The first thing you should do is to confirm the address of the courthouse. This should be on the paperwork given to you by the police, but if not, you can just do a quick search online.

Once you know where you need to go, you can do some quick research to confirm either where to park or how to get there by public transport.

PART 5
THE DAY OF COURT

Once you know more information about your charges and have taken steps to prepare for your court appearance, the next stage is to go to court and appear in front of the Magistrate.

This section outlines all the practical tips you need to know to make your day in court run as smoothly as possible.

What To Wear

It is crucial that you make the best impression possible on the Magistrate, which will help you get a better outcome.

One of the easiest ways to make a good impression is to dress appropriately. This will show the Magistrate that you are taking the process seriously and showing the court the respect it deserves.

Dressing neatly is one of the easiest ways to help your case. Do not wear shorts, thongs or singlets as these are too casual. Also, you should not walk into any courtroom wearing a hat, hoodie or sunglasses. This is likely to irritate the Magistrate and may negatively affect your case.

If you have visible tattoos or facial piercings, you may also want to cover them as much as possible. Even though I have no personal issues with peoples' appearances, and it shouldn't make any difference, some Magistrates may prejudge you based on how you look. The last thing you want is to be given a harsher punishment simply because the Magistrate makes incorrect assumptions based on your appearance.

When To Arrive

You must turn up to court on time. If you are late for court, even by a couple of minutes, it can create serious problems and limit your options.

There is a chance that the Magistrate could deal with the case in your absence, if the court is satisfied you were properly notified. This means that the Magistrate will proceed with your case and sentence you without you even being in court. The main problem is that you never get an opportunity to present your side of the story, or to explain to the Magistrate why your sentence should be reduced.

Another possibility is that the Magistrate could assume that you will not be coming to court at all and issue a warrant for your arrest. If the police then pick you up on an arrest warrant, you could be taken to a police station and held in custody until released.

While missing a court date is serious, in many cases the situation can be fixed if action is taken quickly.

If you have a lawyer representing you, they should contact you a few days before court to confirm when and where you should meet them.

However, if you have decided to appear in court without a lawyer, you will have to check what time you are due to appear in court yourself.

If the police gave you a Notice to Appear, it should tell you what time to arrive at court. Otherwise, you can contact the courthouse you will appear in, and they can check their records to confirm what time your case is likely to start.

As a general rule, you should arrive at 8:30 a.m. to be ready when court starts at 9 a.m.

Be prepared, though – defendants with lawyers always get priority. Even if you get to court at 8:30 a.m., your case may only be heard late in the morning or even in the early afternoon if you are representing yourself.

When I appear in court with my clients, we are sometimes finished by 9:10 a.m. I often walk past the courtroom hours later and still see non-represented defendants waiting for their turn in court.

What To Do When You Arrive

If you have a lawyer representing you, they should have already told you where to meet them on the day of court. They will then guide you through the process and take care of all the steps necessary before appearing in court.

Otherwise, there are several steps to go through when you arrive at court if you are representing yourself.

The first thing you will most likely have to do is go through security. Some courthouses simply have a security guard that you will need to speak to. Other courthouses have walk-through metal detectors and X-ray machines to examine anything you have brought to court.

After going through security, you will need to find your courtroom and let the staff know that you have arrived. Some courthouses have support staff that will tick your name off the list. Otherwise, you will need to speak with the Police Prosecutor who will be presenting your case to the Magistrate. The Prosecutor will most likely be in the courtroom already, so you may have to wait in line to speak with them.

When you speak with the court support person or the Prosecutor, they will ask you what you intend to do with your case. You will then need to take a seat until they call your name.

People who are represented by lawyers have priority. Therefore, if you represent yourself, you will have an opportunity to watch lawyers present their clients' cases. Once they have finished, non-represented people will be called up, and it will be your chance to speak to the Magistrate and explain why you should be given leniency.

Manners in Court

There are some basic manners that you should follow when you enter a courtroom. Depending on the Magistrate, not following these manners could result in anything from the Magistrate politely asking you to comply, all the way through to a Magistrate charging you with contempt of court.

Therefore, if you want to make the best impression possible while in court, I strongly recommend that you follow these simple steps:

1. Bow to the Magistrate as you enter and leave the courtroom.
2. Stand whenever the Magistrate enters or leaves the courtroom or whenever they are speaking to you.

3. Call the Magistrate "Your Honour". Whatever you do, don't call a Magistrate "mate". For obvious reasons, this is strongly discouraged.
4. Turn off your mobile phone. It is not enough to merely put it on silent as it could still make noises for other reasons, for example, if an alarm goes off. I have personally witnessed Magistrates who have confiscated ringing phones which can only be collected again when court closes (usually at 4 p.m.).
5. Don't eat, drink or chew gum.
6. Don't talk while in court. If you need to speak to someone, you should briefly leave the courtroom and then return when you have finished. The courtrooms are small, which means that the Magistrate will likely be able to hear you, even if you are just whispering.
7. Take off hats, caps and sunglasses (religious headwear is fine).

You should also be aware that unless you are part of the media or have specific permission, it is illegal to record proceedings while inside a courtroom. This includes both audio and visual recordings.

PART 6
AFTER COURT

Congratulations – you've made it through court! But that doesn't mean that all the hard work has finished.

Depending on the sentence imposed on you by the Magistrate, you may have further obligations that you need to comply with.

Comply with Court Orders

If you have been sentenced to any penalty that requires you to take any steps after court, you must comply with the orders made.

Some of these can be:

- Don't drive if your driver's licence has been disqualified;
- Report to a Probation or Parole Office if required; or
- Sign a recognisance.

If you are unsure whether you were meant to do anything after you finished in court, you can attend the courthouse registry and ask them to check the file to confirm any obligations you might have had.

Pay Fines or Restitution/Compensation Orders

If you were ordered to pay a fine or a restitution/compensation order, you will need to make arrangements to pay this. In many cases, the amount will automatically be referred to SPER for collection. If not, you will have been given a period of time to pay the amount.

It will be up to you to make the necessary arrangements but, at the very least, I recommend that you make sure that the courthouse and/or SPER have your correct contact details. The last thing you want is to not receive the notice telling you how to pay the outstanding amount and then getting into further trouble because you have failed to make payment as required.

Seek Legal Advice About Appealing

Although it doesn't happen very often, sometimes Magistrates get things wrong. They are, after all, human just like you and me.

Most people will never need to appeal a sentence. This information is included so you understand your rights, not because appeals are common.

The worst-case scenario is that a Magistrate has misunderstood either the facts of your case or the laws that apply. In these situations, you could end up with a much worse sentence than it should have been and could even result in you being unlawfully imprisoned.

This is why the criminal justice system allows a person to appeal their sentence to a higher court. In the case of Magistrates Court cases, an appeal will first be heard in the District Court and can then be further appealed to the Court of Appeal, if required.

An appeal involves a Judge reviewing a sentence imposed by a Magistrate and then deciding whether that sentence was correct. If the Judge decides that the sentence was appropriate, they will refuse to make any changes. If, however, a Judge decides that there has been an error, they can impose their own sentence that they think is fair or send the case back to the Magistrates Court so that the person can be appropriately resentenced.

You should, however, be aware that a Judge might decide that a sentence was incorrect but then decide that the Magistrate was, in fact, too lenient on you. If that happens, you will end up with a more severe punishment than what was imposed by the Magistrate.

An appeal is a highly complex process, and you should not consider starting one without speaking to a lawyer first. They will review what happened in court and will then be able to provide advice on your prospects of a successful appeal.

FREQUENTLY ASKED QUESTIONS

I am often asked the same questions by people who are representing themselves. To assist, I have answered some of the more common questions below.

Can the Court provide Legal Advice?

Only a lawyer can provide you with legal advice.

Magistrates and Prosecutors are not allowed to provide you with any legal advice. The most they can do is give you some procedural advice (for example, where to sign a bail undertaking).

Suppose a Prosecutor tries to give you legal advice. In that case, you can take into account what they tell you but do not rely on this information until you have spoken with a defence lawyer.

Am I Eligible for Legal Aid Funding?

If you want a lawyer to represent you but cannot afford to pay their fees, you may be able to apply for assistance from Legal Aid Queensland, a service funded and operated by the Queensland government.

Legal Aid Queensland can provide free legal advice in some simple cases. However, for anything more complex, they may be able to provide funding for a lawyer to represent you.

To be eligible for Legal Aid funding, you must show that you meet the funding tests and that your case is serious enough. In most cases, you need to be able to show that you are at risk of imprisonment.

To find out if you are eligible for Legal Aid funding, you can contact Legal Aid Queensland to discuss.

Can Someone Speak for me in Court?

As a general rule, the only person who can speak on your behalf is your lawyer. I have seen many parents or spouses try to talk to the Magistrate on behalf of their loved one, only to be told (sometimes not very politely) to take a seat.

There are, however, a few exceptions.

If you struggle to understand spoken English because it is not your first language, you may be able to have an interpreter speak on your behalf. However, this does not mean that the interpreter can say whatever they want – all they can do is directly translate what you tell them and what the Magistrate or Prosecutor says in court. Therefore, you will still need to speak in court even if you are using an interpreter.

If you are under the care of a medical professional, particularly for your mental health, a Magistrate may also allow that professional to discuss your situation in court.

Some Magistrates are much more relaxed about who speaks in court. Even though it is not common, some Magistrates will speak with family members or other support people present in court.

Missing a Court Date

If you miss a court date, the consequences can be severe.

The Magistrate may have already dealt with the case in your absence or may have issued a warrant for your arrest in the worst-case scenario.

If you think you might have missed a court date, the first step is to contact a lawyer specialising in criminal law.

When I am contacted by someone who thinks they may have missed a court date, I contact both the courthouse registry and the Police Prosecutors to determine what happened on the day of court.

Depending on the result, I will then take whatever steps are necessary to fix the issue. This could be anything from arranging for a closed case to be reopened to go through the sentencing steps properly, to helping a person surrender to court to have the arrest warrant cancelled.

If you think you've missed a court date, act quickly. The longer you leave it, the worse the consequences can be.

Changing the Court Location

When the police charge you with an offence, they will tell you which courthouse you must appear in – this will usually be the closest courthouse to where the offence took place.

Sometimes, however, it can be difficult for a person to appear in the allocated courthouse. For example, a person living in Brisbane may have been charged with possessing drugs while on holiday in Cairns. That person would then be required to fly back up to Cairns for their case and then return to Brisbane at a high cost to them.

In these situations, we can apply to the courthouse for a case to be transferred to the closest courthouse to where our clients live. In the above example, we would apply for the drugs case to be transferred to Brisbane.

You should be aware, however, that a transfer request will only be accepted if a person is pleading guilty to the offence. The courthouse may also have a general policy not to transfer cases to other courthouses for other reasons.

If you would like to find out more about transferring your case to a different courthouse, you should seek legal advice.

How long will your case take from start to finish?

If you are charged with a traffic or criminal offence, you will be given a court date that will usually be 3-4 weeks after being charged. Depending on the circumstances, it could be shorter or longer than this.

If your case is not particularly lengthy or complex and if you have already done everything necessary to prepare, you should be able to finalise your case on the first court appearance.

However, if you are not ready to proceed, you can ask the court for an "adjournment". An adjournment is simply a request to come back in a few weeks so that you have more time to get everything prepared. If you want to adjourn so that you can hire a lawyer, you can ask for an adjournment specifically to seek legal advice.

Most Magistrates will grant one adjournment without needing to be convinced. However, if you are asking for a second or third adjournment, they will want to know what is causing the delay.

If you have a lawyer appearing in court with you, they will make the adjournment application on your behalf. You are also more likely to be granted additional adjournments if your lawyer is making the requests, as the Magistrate will trust that your lawyer is progressing your case appropriately.

Are the Media Allowed in Court?

One of the questions I am asked the most is whether the media are allowed in court. This is not surprising, as most people do not want their cases to be discussed online or in other media.

Unfortunately, in most cases, the answer is yes – the media are allowed in court. The only exception is if the Magistrate has granted an application to exclude the media, which only happens in exceptional circumstances.

Therefore, if you are due to appear in court, you need to be prepared that the media may report on your case.

In addition, each courthouse publishes a list of everyone who is due to appear in court that day. This is known as the Daily Law List and is publicly available on the Queensland Courts website.

I have noticed that these lists often show up in internet search results. This means that your name might appear in a search result, therefore revealing that you were required to attend a certain courthouse on a particular date.

Fortunately, the Daily Law Lists do not provide any further details, such as why you are required to attend court or what the outcome was.

What is Bail?

Bail is a written promise that you sign confirming that you will attend court on a particular date. This allows you to remain in the community until your case is finished.

In many cases, the police will grant you bail after you have been arrested and charged. However, if the police refuse to grant bail, you will need to apply to a Magistrate for bail.

To determine whether to grant bail, the Magistrate will look at the seriousness of your offences and your previous history. They will also consider other factors such as the risk of you offending again or interfering with witnesses.

If you can convince the Magistrate that you are not a risk, you should be granted bail.

As always, it is best to seek legal advice if you are concerned about bail.

How Can I Get a Record of the Sentence?

At some point after you have finished your court case, you may need to get a letter from the court confirming the outcome.

You can contact the courthouse registry and request a "Verdict and Judgment Record". This document will outline the details of your sentencing, including:

- The offences you were convicted of;
- Your sentencing date;
- The courthouse you appeared in;
- The name of the Magistrate who sentenced you; and
- The penalty you received.

The court registry may impose a small fee to provide this paperwork. However, it is an official record of your court outcome, so it can be an important document to have.

NEXT STEPS

By now, you should have a good understanding of how to prepare for court and what to do when you get there. The information provided in this book will have put you on the right path for getting through this challenging stage in your life.

For most readers of this book, you will now have three options:

1. You can take what you have learned from this book and represent yourself in court. Even though many people do this every day, there is a genuine risk that you may receive a harsher outcome than necessary.
2. You can obtain free legal advice from a community legal centre and then represent yourself. You will be much better off than if you had not taken any steps to prepare but you may still end up with a worse-than-necessary punishment.
3. You can obtain legal representation. Working with a lawyer is, without a doubt, the best option if you want to give yourself the best chance possible of a good outcome. If you are eligible, you can apply to Legal Aid Queensland for Government-funded representation. Otherwise, you can hire a lawyer privately, which will give you the highest level of legal representation.

How you choose to proceed from here is up to you.

Regardless of the decision you make, I hope you have found this information useful and that it helps you to survive the court process.

If I can be of service to you, please let me know. I wish you all the best as you move forward.

If you would like to discuss your situation or understand your options before court, you can contact my team at help@harperfinch.com.au.

Dave Abrey

ABOUT DAVE ABREY

Dave is a Brisbane-based criminal defence lawyer and the Principal Lawyer of Harper Finch Lawyers.

For nearly two decades, he has represented thousands of clients charged with offences ranging from drink driving and assault to serious indictable matters, appearing in courts across Queensland, including the Court of Appeal.

Dave is known for his clear, practical approach to the criminal justice system - explaining complex court processes in a way that reduces fear, confusion, and costly mistakes for people facing court for the first time. His experience has seen him invited to speak at TEDxBrisbane and regularly contribute commentary to media outlets on criminal law and court processes.

Outside the courtroom, Dave is an endurance athlete. In 2019, he ran the length of Tasmania over five consecutive days to raise funds for the Charlie Teo Foundation, averaging 60 kilometres a day.

This book brings together everything Dave has learned from thousands of court appearances - written for people who want to walk into court informed, prepared, and confident.

Made in the USA
Monee, IL
04 November 2026

67374662R00039